DESERTS

SIMON & SCHUSTER

LONDON • SYDNEY • NEW YORK • TOKYO • SINGAPORE • TORONTO

Author Dr. Brian Knapp
Illustrator Mark Franklin
Designed and produced by
EARTHSCAPE EDITIONS,
86 Peppard Road,
Sonning Common, Reading,
Berkshire, RG4 9RP, UK

First Published in 1991 by
Simon & Schuster Young Books
Simon & Schuster Ltd
Wolsey House
Wolsey Road
Hemel Hempstead
Hertfordshire HP2 4SS
England

Copyright © 1991 by Simon & Schuster
Young Books

British Library Cataloguing in Publication Data

Knapp, Brian
    Deserts (Caring for environments)
    1. Deserts – Juvenile literature
    I. Title   II. Series
    551.4

    ISBN 0-7500-0843-1

Printed and bound in Hong Kong

CONTENTS

1: WHAT ARE THE DESERTS?

Deserts – places where more water is lost through evaporation than falls as rain – cover a third of the Earth's land surface. They have been shunned by people because they are harsh and inhospitable. Yet they are lands where an enormous variety of life exists.

Deserts are places of great landscape beauty. Here you will find some of the most awesome cliffs, highest mountains, vast empty plains and spectacular dawns and sunsets.

People cannot easily live in these lands. It has taken thousands of years of acclimatization and experience for the desert-dwellers to be able to survive and prosper. But many inexperienced people have tried to conquer the desert. They have been drawn by the possibility of farming if only they could find water, and the chance of being immensely rich if only they could find the mineral ores that lie near the surface.

Some countries have used their wealth to turn desert into city, others have come to enjoy the sunny dry weather – and pay to have air conditioning brought to their homes. Few have tried to live on the desert's terms.

Three quarters of the world's deserts have bare rock or stones at the surface. But they contain many surprises. The rocks in the background to this picture, for example, may look barren and inhospitable, but they hide water that forms a spring and provides enough water to support the palm trees.

These resources are small and easily over-exploited and people have to be especially careful if they use them.

Sand covers only a quarter of the world's deserts. But sand is the most inhospitable of all environments. Sand seas are almost impossible to cross or to live in. In most countries the sand seas are virtually uninhabited. Yet a shower will give enough moisture for plants to flower, even on sand.

__The desert has a long memory.__ The car looks as though it has been recently abandoned instead of over 20 years ago. The shack in the background was last used nearly a century ago, yet it still stands intact. In a dry environment with little to cause rusting or rotting, the scars produced by the unthinking acts of people will remain in the landscape for perhaps thousands of years.

How people have survived in the desert, what uses can be made of it, and how we can preserve these beautiful lands for future generations to enjoy, depends on understanding how the desert has formed. This is described in the first part of this book. The second part of the book describes how people have tried to live in the desert and why they have sometimes been defeated by it. The final part is about how we can look after the desert, especially in areas which are under great pressure from people.

__Nature may be under great pressure__ in a desert, but it is far from defeated and a wide variety of living things thrive. With little water plants grow sparsely and slowly. All animals therefore need large territories just to gather enough food for their needs.

Recognizing deserts

An average of two hundred and fifty millimetres of rainfall a year is sometimes used to mark the desert boundaries of the world. But it is not so much the amount of rain that decides where the desert boundary will be. Instead deserts are produced by *irregular and unreliable rainfall* and where, on balance, *the amount of rain that falls cannot match the ground's ability to evaporate it.*

This picture shows many features of deserts throughout the world. Sand dunes with their sparse vegetation make up the low-lying foreground. Beyond is a plain covered in stones and backed by stoney slopes. But most of the landscape is rocky and barren, with craggy profiles and numerous deeply etched valleys.

Deserts can be identified by looking at the way winds and water operate, and noticing how wildlife has adapted to the environment through millions of years of evolution.

Deserts are best thought of as places where plants and animals are sparse and scattered, and where each living thing is highly adapted to coping with months or even years without rainfall and yet is able to take advantage of brief torrential rain whenever it falls.

The world's deserts

The largest areas of natural deserts – called **arid zones** – stretch across each continent between latitudes 20° and 40°. Theses are the hot climatic deserts.

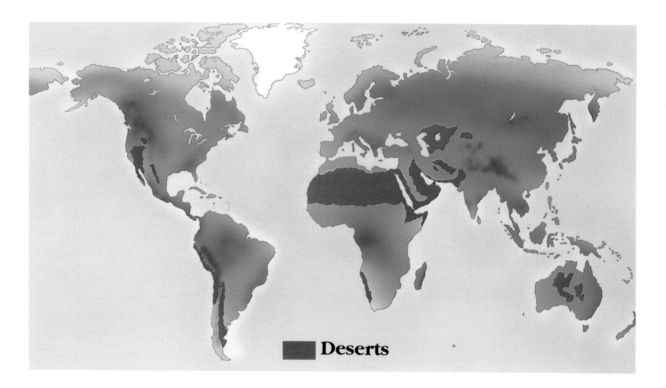

Deserts

The world's deserts

They are so dry because they do not receive any moisture-bearing winds. They occur below the world's permanent **high pressure** regions. In these parts of the world air sinks and spreads out giving an intensely dry, warm climate. Rain only falls when the high pressure breaks down for short periods and allows the advance of moist air from nearby regions.

Deserts are also found in the shelter of high mountain ranges such as the Andes of South America and the Sierra Nevada of North America. These barriers act like wringers, forcing moist air to rise and shed its moisture before it reaches the valleys and plains beyond. These are known as **rainshadow** deserts. Finally cold deserts occupy the extreme Arctic areas. Here it is the cold, more than the lack of moisture, that limits life. Indeed moisture – in the form of snow and ice – is often abundant.

The margins

Deserts rarely have sharp boundaries. Instead the conditions that give a desert gradually give way to more moist environments. Places of transition from true deserts are often called **semi-arid zones**.

Semi-arid zones generally have a season, usually summer, when rainfall is more reliable. Thunderstorms occur each year and enough moisture is stored in the soil for a greater variety of shrubs and trees to grow. They are called such names as 'the outback' (in Australia) and 'the Sahel' (in Africa).

Semi-arid zones are still regions of intense drought and unreliable rainfall. But, whereas everyone can tell that a true desert is a difficult place to live, many people have been unwisely tempted to try to scratch a living from marginal regions. We shall see the tragedy this has caused later in this book.

2: DESERT WEATHER

Deserts are places of uncertainty – no-one can easily say when the next rain might fall or how long it will last. Months and even years may pass between storms and then torrential rain may fall for days on end. It is this uncertainty that both wildlife and people have to adapt to.

The tropical deserts are clearly seen in this satellite picture. Where the air rises and produces rain there are thick white clouds. Where it sinks again the clouds disappear and the sky is clear. Because they are cloud-free for much of the year, deserts are usually the easiest land areas to pick out on a satellite image.

Where air sinks

Desert air is not only rain-free, but dry. A reservoir might lose a metre thickness of water from its surface in a hot desert. Soils become parched until they are as dry as dust.

Just as rain forms when moist air rises and cools to give clouds in some parts of the world, so air must sink elsewhere to keep a balance over the Earth. Deserts are places where air sinks, and as it does so it becomes warmer and drier.

The major places where the air sinks are on the edges of the Tropics. Here the weather charts are labelled HIGH pressure to show that the air is sinking. It sinks here to balance rising air near the equator. The only time that rain falls is when the sinking air is nudged out of the way. When this happens all the heat stored in the ground causes violent storms to release torrents of rain.

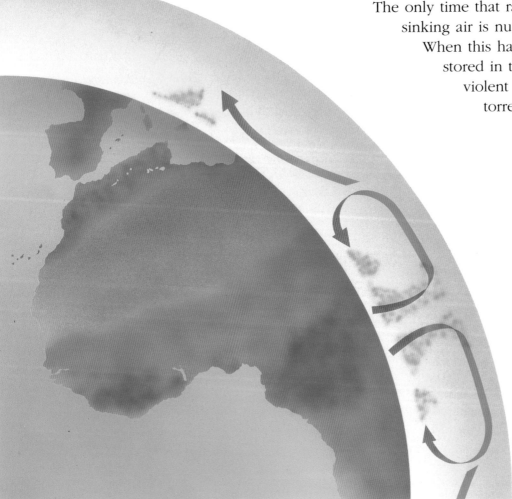

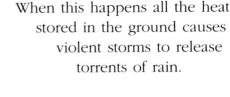

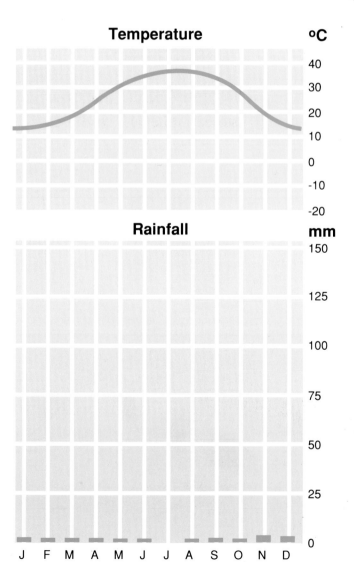

Mountain barrier

Mountains can cause warm air to fall, but on a smaller scale. A large mountain range is a huge obstacle to the Earth's winds. To get over it the air has to squash and rise. This forces the air to cool and shed much of its moisture.

Once past the barrier the air expands and sinks again. Now deprived of most of its moisture, the air is very unlikely to produce rain, no matter how much it might rise again.

Temperature °C

40
30
20
10
0
-10
-20

Rainfall mm

150

125

100

75

50

25

0

J F M A M J J A S O N D

The Andes are a formidable barrier to moist air. In this picture taken from space you can see how huge swirls of air pile up against the side of the Andes yet most get no further than the continent's edge. The inland mountains and plains are made into deserts

Making sense of desert records

Average statistics never give a true picture of a desert. This is a climate graph for Ain Salah, a remote town in the northern edge of Sahara desert in Africa. Rainfall is almost non-existent, and temperature appears to be constant. Yet every day the temperature changes by over 20°C and the rain falls in rare but torrential showers.

Weather of extremes

Deserts hold most of the world records for weather extremes. They have the heaviest rainstorms, the longest droughts, the highest daytime temperatures and the biggest temperature range in a day. High mountain deserts are also some of the coldest places at night.

The weather of clear skies

Cloud acts like a blanket within the air. It shelters the land from the harshest heat of the Sun during the day, and stops the heat of the Earth leaving quickly at night.

People struggling homeward in a dust storm.
Notice how there is little vegetation to hold the dusty soil in check.

Places that commonly have cloud therefore get only a small change in temperature between the day and the night. In the deserts, where the clouds rarely occur, the Sun beats down on the land: this makes the deserts nearest the tropics the hottest places on Earth. At night the clear sky allows the heat to radiate out to space and temperatures plummet. As a result, it is not at all unusual for desert nights to be frosty.

The cool nights have many advantages for the wildlife of the deserts. Most animals are nocturnal, seeking their food in the relative cool of the night and then hiding and sleeping in burrows during the heat of the day. Plants also do some of their collecting at night, but in this case they collect moisture that may have accumulated as **dew** in the cooling air.

This rare sight is a small flash flood. The river bed to the right is dry. Somewhere a few kilometres away a thunderstorm is making a river whose leading edge is arriving as a wall of water on the left.

Traditional desert clothing gives a clear picture of the weather that has to be endured. People from the world's hottest places cover their bodies to protect them from the searing heat of the Sun by day and to keep themselves warm by night. The loose folds of their clothes are ideal for such contrasts. The head-dress that many people wear is suited not just to protect the head from the Sun but its folds can also be drawn around the face to keep out the dust from the frequent wind-driven sand and dust storms.

When it rains

Rain comes to a desert as a torrential downpour. The downpour might be from a single thunderstorm and last just an hour or two; more rarely it is from a mass of moist air that will give rain for several days at a time.

Much of the desert has just a thin skin of sand or rubble over hard rock. None of it is enough to soak up the rain that falls. Within seconds of a downpour the water is cascading over the rocks and down steep ravines. But often it is hardly recognizable as water. Instead it is a dirty brown colour, filled with the sand and dust of the desert.

As the winds blow

There are many causes for the hot winds that blow incessantly across many deserts. Many are driven in part by the heat of the day and at night the land is calm. Others blow over huge regions as part of the general circulation of the atmosphere. The open, vegetation-free land provides little shelter and hardly resists the flow of air so that it sometimes becomes powerful enough to pick up dust and sand and create the much-feared desert dust and sandstorms.

3: DESERT LANDFORMS

Over three thousand years ago the Egyptians began their great monuments in one of the driest places on Earth. Today the monuments the ancient Egyptians built have not crumbled away as they would have done in more humid places.

These statues are good timekeepers. They tell us that the rocks of deserts crumble, or weather, slowly. The fact that the deserts show some of the most exciting natural sculptures on Earth simply points to the long time deserts have been in the making. In some places it must also point to change. The lands we now see as deserts may have been much wetter in the distant past. What we now see are virtually fossilized lands.

__Monument Valley__ , Utah, is a rock desert that has been formed by millions of years of slow erosion. The tall masses of rock are called buttes. You can see that, even as they waste away and are reduced to mere needles of rock, they keep their cliff-like faces. Even the valley floor has little __debris__ . The bareness of the land tells us that the rate at which nature can carry rock fragments from a desert by wind, and occasionally water, is faster than new debris can be formed.

The Abu Simbell statues

These fantastic sculptures from Ancient Egypt lie high up on a desert cliff, far from any sea. Their near perfect condition indicates how little weathering has taken place in over three thousand years.

Sharp shapes

Deserts are marked by their angular landforms. There is no soil and plant carpet to soften the shape.

Some of the most striking desert features are majestic cliffs and vast level plains. They are especially common where the rock has been laid down in parallel flat sheets.

Here it is easy to see the way that natural processes wear the landscape away. The whole cliff is exposed to the weather. Water, and sometimes even frost, combine to prise slabs of rock away along its natural fissures.

As each slab crashes to the ground it breaks into smaller pieces. Here they lie, littering the slope below until they are broken down into fine particles that can be washed away by storms or blown away by the wind.

Meanwhile newly exposed cliff rocks are attacked by the forces of weathering. In this way the cliff retreats back, its steep face always keeping the same angle, no matter how little cliff remains.

This natural arch shows the way that natural processes can wear away some types of desert cliffs, grain by grain. Here two **canyons** have been formed close to each other, and the valley wall between is very thin.

As each valley wall weathered, so it retreated back towards the other. Eventually they met, and for a few hundred or a few thousand years this spectacular arch will remain.

Where the cliff edges are fretted by deep parallel canyons they leave promontories called mesas.

As the mesas are made smaller by erosion they sometimes leave remnant islands called buttes, or pinnacles called needle rocks.

Surviving intact to the last, these needles of rock are at the end of a mesa. The skirt below the cliff is made of shale. Shale rock (a form of clay) is easily eroded and cannot easily form steep sided cliffs.

Water's torrential power

Water is not a frequent visitor to desert lands. But when a rainstorm bursts it can flood the land with cascading water in a matter of minutes. At these times the thin **veneer** of sands and gravels that are strewn over the hillsides are easily carried away because there are no plant roots to bind them in place. As a result, just an hour's rain once every few years can easily carry away all the material that weathering has been able to loosen since the previous storm.

Rainstorms in a desert do not give enough water to sustain a normal river. Observers have sometimes likened a desert river in **spate** to liquid cement moving at the speed of an express train. But the rushing torrent and debris is quickly spent. The water cannot travel very far in this short time and it soon soaks into the

Desert valleys – called arroyos or canyons – have steep barren sides and flat floors. When rain falls there is nothing to soak it up and soon cascades down to the valley, creating a flash flood. The flat floor of the valley becomes choked with debris washed off the slopes. The debris may be tens or even hundreds of metres thick.

The junction between a mountain front and a plain is marked by gently sloping fans of debris. As soon as the flash floods leave the confines of the mountains their waters spread out and soak away. Within a kilometre or two of the mountain front the coarse debris is deposited forming into a fan.

Fans are giant features when seen from close to. The picture here shows the most recent channel cut into the surface of a fan. It is so big the slope hardly shows at all.

gravels of the valley bottoms, adding further layers to the material strewn there from previous storms.

When the water from a flash flood moves onto flat land the debris it has brought with it is then deposited.

Permanent water

You have to look hard for water in a desert, but there are few deserts in the world that do not have some reliable supply. At first a landscape may not look very promising. You may see a wide and apparently desolate basin which appears to be home to only the hardiest of plants. But if you let your eye move to the lowest point, you will see that there is a white region. Move closer and the white patch becomes a lake. And even in the driest periods when the white of encrusted salt covers the lake bed, you are sure to find some water.

Fresh water

The trouble with desert lake water is that it is **saline**. As the water soaked slowly through the rocks it dissolved some of their minerals and carried them in solution to accumulate at the lowest point in the landscape. So much desert water is of no use to plants, animals or people.

This basin landscape is an ideal place to look for a playa lake. When rain falls onto the surrounding hills it cascades down and soaks into the basin sands. There it seeps down to the lowest levels in the basin centre. If there is enough water it rises to the surface and forms a lake. When this picture was taken the lake was nearly dry but its extent was still marked by brilliant white salt crusts.

Water that has seeped through rocks has often picked up so many minerals that it is useless for irrigation or for drinking. As the water in these desert salt lakes evaporates it leaves behind a white salt scum. This is the famous salt lake in California's Death Valley desert. Its name tells you exactly how useful it is.

Sources of fresh water are much rarer. Many rocks lie in continuous sheets that can stretch over thousands of square kilometres. So although a layer of limestone or sandstone rock may be buried beneath the driest deserts, elsewhere it may form an exposed ridge in a rainfed mountain.

Water-bearing rocks are called **aquifers.** You cannot spot an aquifer by the shape of the land surface, but occasionally the water will rise naturally as a spring and give rise to a patch of land where plants can get reliable supplies of nourishment. Such places are called **oases**.

Rivers in the desert

Desert rivers are rare. They must have their sources in distant lands where there is water every year and they must be substantial enough to survive passing through a region where the river bed and banks are parched and thirsty. Small rivers soon dry up in a desert.

You can just see the thin blue trail of the River Colorado as it winds its way through the centre of the Grand Canyon in Arizona, USA. But although there is much water in the river it does little to relieve the desert, where the parched surface lies nearly two kilometres above the river bed.

Some of the world's large rivers flow through deserts. The Niger in West Africa, the Colorado in the USA and the Nile in Egypt are all examples of rivers that have their sources in a rainy climate but which flow through deserts.

But although a river may flow for hundreds of kilometres in a desert, the water will make little difference to the parched land. The main effect of a desert river, however, is to create a deep valley. This happens because the river cuts into the floor of the valley at a faster rate than the sides of the valley.

Seas of sand

Of all the desert's remarkable features, perhaps the most spectacular are the regions of sand. Here dunes pile on dunes often as far as the eye can see. The peoples of the Sahara desert call these places 'ergs', which means seas of sand.

Where sand settles

Sand seas usually form where the desert is flat. They are mounds of ground-down rock blown together by the wind, just like coastal sand dunes are piles of sand blown from beaches.

Sand grains are too big to be lifted far from the ground even by strong winds and so they hop and bounce along at up to a metre from the surface. This kind of movement is called **saltation**.

The wind forms the sand into many kinds of regular patterns. The smallest are called ripples; there may be ten ripples to a metre. The ripples rest on the back of larger features called dunes. These form in long lines with complex shapes.

Sand is driven up the ramp of a dune by the wind, then it falls over the top and collapses in a straight, steep slope. This gives many dunes a sharp-crested edge.

The tops of sand dunes often snake across the landscape and one dune ridge may intertwine with another. Sometimes the sand dunes pile up and make pyramids of sand that can be over 100 metres high. These are called sand mountains.

Dunes are constantly on the march, being driven by the wind. Their advance is most clear when they move towards places where trees grow, as shown in this picture. If the dunes are very big they will eventually overwhelm the trees and move on; if the dunes are small the trees may check their advance.

Sand dunes are both loose and firm. They are made of loose grains that are easily moved as shown by the footprints in the picture on the left. This is what allows sand to be blown about. But sand also compacts into strong shapes, supporting the walker and allowing dunes to form.

DESERT LANDFORMS

4: NATURE IN THE DESERT

Nowhere on Earth is too inhospitable for nature – and this includes the desert. It might be an environment of extremes, but evolution has made sure that some living things can survive.

No desert is free of vegetation. Only patches of rapidly moving sand dunes can be plant-free. Elsewhere plants cling tenaciously to tiny cracks in the rock where some soil has formed, or they sink roots tens of metres deep to tap the moisture far below the surface. All the plants and animals have special means of adapting to irregular rainfall. Plants grow slowly and carefully. They reserve their energies to deal with natural threats. Animals are specialist feeders. They are each adapted to feed from just a small range of plants. But there are penalties to these strategies: wild species are poorly prepared to cope with trampling and grazing from goats and cattle, or changes in land use. Once a desert wilderness is harmed it will not recover for many generations to come. Once desert wildlife is displaced it may be lost forever.

Making the best use of its resources, this plant stores all its food in its bulbous stem to make the flowers and seeds that will ensure a new generation.

The cactus – a type of plant known as a succulent – stores water in its thick fleshy stem. The spines are its leaves and are also used for protection. The cactus has quite a small root network and this runs mainly near the surface. The job of the roots is to gather any rain that soaks into the soil and then transfer it to the stem where it can be stored until the rain comes again.

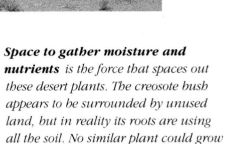

Space to gather moisture and nutrients *is the force that spaces out these desert plants. The creosote bush appears to be surrounded by unused land, but in reality its roots are using all the soil. No similar plant could grow next to it and be able to survive.*

Plants growing close to one another use different parts of the soil, but they are still at a distance from one another.

There are two ways of dealing with drought.
One is to send down deep roots that can tap the last reserves of moisture that lie deep in the soil. Plants that grow in stream beds or in valley bottoms often use this strategy. The other way is to spread roots far and wide near to the surface and then hold the moisture that falls in surface stems or underground tubers. Plants of rock-strewn slopes often cope this way.

The plant in this picture shows how appearances can be deceiving. On the surface it looks like a small bush with tiny leathery leaves and hard thin branches. Here the purpose is to prevent moisture loss by **transpiration** *in the scorching sun.*

But you only see a part on the surface. Below ground is a tap root that plunges deep down in the search for water. Large plants can send tap roots for tens of metres and even penetrate the cracks within rocks. A network of roots spreads at every level in the soil to gather whatever nutriment that may be around.

Criss cross trails *etched in sand give a vivid impression of the wide variety of desert life.*

Hunt and be hunted *is the deadly game that goes on at night. The beetle out on a forage for dead vegetable matter to eat may well fall prey to a scorpion, a night-time hunter that spends its days under rocks.*

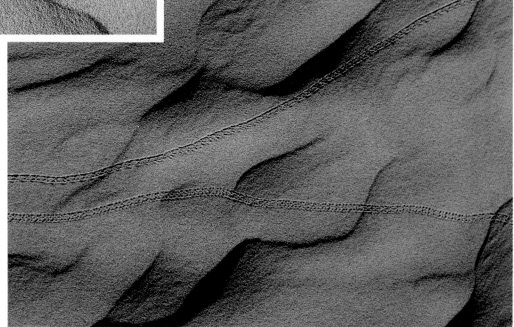

Camels have many adaptations *to survive in the desert. They have special hooves that spread their weight and stop them sinking in the sand. They are able to drink tens of litres of water when they find it and then go for several days without needing any more. They are able to chew the hardest and least appetizing leaves and their stomachs will get every last piece of nutrient from them.*

5: FARMING THE DESERT

Even a desert offers a livelihood for people – provided that they understand the way Nature works. In this part of the book we shall look at how people have successfully lived with the desert for thousands of years because they understand the limits it imposes. We shall also see why some people have been forced to put more and more pressure on desert margins, and how water is not the answer to desert survival.

Dates, eaten fresh or dried for storage, are a well-known product of some varieties of palm tree. Date palms can grow using soil water that would be too salty for most other plants.

The palms can be used for many other products as well. The leaves will make fodder, thatch and string, and the trunks can be used for building or fuel. However, palm trees grow slowly. It may take over a century for a palm to grow to replace one cut down. This is why harvesting the desert needs great care.

Herding animals is a time consuming activity. With no fences to keep the animals in one place people have to be constantly on their guard for straying animals. In this way traditional farming keeps many members of a family occupied.

Hunting and gathering

All over the world desert peoples have learned the art of successful survival by simply using the food that the desert provides. They live in harmony with nature, taking only what can be replaced. They are called hunter-gatherers.

Herders

Another way of using the desert is to rely on grazing animals such as camels or goats. These resourceful grazers can use even the most unpromising plant as food. Herders tend to rely on their animals for all their needs: milk, meat and hides. But animals need a large amount of space to graze and water to drink. Herders have to find water for their animals and so they prefer land near water-holes and areas on desert margins.

On the move

In a place like a desert food is thin on the ground. Even the most resourceful people soon find the most accessible roots, the most obvious burrows, and the resting places of animals. After this, life gets harder and it is time to move to a new area. People who have no fixed home but move from one area to another in search of food either by hunter-gathering or with herds of animals are called nomads.

It is easy to imagine that the camel trains that traditionally trek across the desert can be independent of their environment. Certainly they are capable of carrying provisions with them. But the camel-train drivers have to be skilled at finding both food and water in an emergency. As a result they tend to know many of the skills of the traditional desert hunter gatherers.

Catch as catch can

Without water it is very difficult to plan for a harvest and the desert will remain a place where just a few may live. But those who persevere can make the most of their opportunities by building walls of stones and sand that will store any rain that falls. Planting seed for corn may stand only one chance in ten of growing. When this is treated as a bonus, the occasional crop can make all the difference between mere survival and a better life.

Oasis dwellers

If it is possible to secure a reliable supply of water the use of a desert can be widened enormously. Natural springs occur even in arid regions if they are fed with water that has flowed through underground rocks from distant rain-fed mountains.

A spring allows water to seep into the surrounding sand and rock, and weathering turns this to soil. A quite different range of plants can now grow. Trees can flourish and even a small forest may develop. These areas of seeping water have traditionally been called oases in Africa, springs in America and billabongs in Australia.

People living near to an oasis can use the water to produce reliable crops. Where palm trees grow they can be harvested for dates. The water can be channelled to provide a constant supply to irrigate small gardens in which vegetables and cereals can be grown.

The difference between the unwatered desert and the water-fed or irrigated desert is astounding. Reliable water turns scratching a living into a life of plenty.

Desert-dwellers know that the best place to catch water is in the bottom of a valley, or wadi, just after a storm. So long as the flash flood is not too ferocious, small walls built across the valley floor will hold back water which can sink into the ground and provide moisture for crops. You can see patterns of small walls in this picture.

The number of people who can live in an oasis depends on how much water they have available. Only a small spring issues from the rocks in this picture. It is sufficient to provide drinking water, but not enough to irrigate the land. So the village remains small and the farmers are mostly herders. If the population of the village grows too large, the surplus young people will have to seek jobs in distant places.

Notice how small walls, or terraces, have been made across the slopes near the village. These are designed to trap any rain that falls. Their purpose is similar to walls in a valley bottom.

Rivers are uncommon in deserts and found only where their sources lie in rain and snow-fed mountains. Some rivers, such as the Colorado in the USA or the Nile in Egypt, are grand rivers, these waters can support huge areas of irrigation. But many others are just big enough to water the valleys in which they flow.

In this Moroccan valley, the flat land beside the river is a sea of date palm trees and small irrigated fields. By contrast, the hillsides around are arid and unproductive.

Making the desert bloom

Because crops grow well in a hot desert when they have sufficient supply of water, many people have come to believe that water is the only key to desert success. But natural springs do not provide enough water for thirsty farmers. Governments therefore have sunk bore-holes down to the aquifers or have even diverted rivers for hundreds or sometimes thousands of kilometres. The result has transformed the productivity of the desert, but at the expense of the natural environment.

Water in the rocks

If aquifers can be reached by digging or drilling a well, they can yield a reliable supply both for drinking and farming in a desert. However, it takes time for water to seep through rocks. In some cases the mountains that were once rain-fed are themselves now parts of immense deserts and they can no longer recharge water taken out of wells and boreholes. This means that taking water from desert rocks is like mining coal from the ground: you can do it until the reserves run out. The animals and crops of many deserts and

Hoover Dam has been heralded as one of the world's modern wonders. It is the most spectacular dam of the many reservoirs that store the Colorado's water. The 180 kilometre long reservoir supplies water for irrigation to farmers for hundreds of kilometres each side of the river, as well as water to desert cities and industry.

An artesian well taps the groundwater of an aquifer. Using this water it is easy to provide irrigation for crops. Here water is sprayed recklessly over crops. The natural desert hills can be seen in the background.

semi-deserts are sustained by this kind of water. It will not last more than a few decades in most cases. Then what will the people do?

Holding water in check

A river that runs unchecked through a desert is often seen as wasted water. People have long sought to dam such rivers and use the stored water to support even more animals and crops. The Egyptians have dammed the Nile to make an inland sea called Lake Nasser which gives a constant and reliable year-round water supply for the country. Likewise, the Americans and Mexicans have dammed the River Colorado to form a string of reservoirs to feed their thirsty deserts.

Harnessed rivers give new opportunities for people to make a livelihood from the desert, but by doing so they are putting the fragile desert under stress. Furthermore, watering the desert to make farmland is never economical. It always costs more to build a desert dam than the farmers pay for the water it holds back.

If they had to pay the proper price the farmers could never afford to grow their crops. So everyone in a country pays a price for the cultivation of the deserts – and the destruction of the natural environment.

Once the water has been brought to a new area simple systems like these **siphon** tubes will take controlled amounts to fields. In this way a desert can grow tomatoes and other water-hungry crops with ease.

It is common to find huge canals winding their way through deserts in developed countries where there is the technology and the money to support water transfer projects. The water can be used to support desert cities or to feed plants that grow quickly in the desert heat.

Desert margin tragedy

Desert, water and people usually don't mix. When people find new water they often get ideas about how to use the desert that can soon exhaust the land. Within a short time they begin to mine the water resources of the desert: the plants, the soil, and the wildlife are all disturbed.

The danger is greatest in the semi-arid desert margins. Here there is a little more rain, a few more trees, and water in the form of wells provides a bit more encouragement for people to stay.

Water, but not quite enough

People can bring water to the desert margins. They can pump it from the ground and make it flow along channels called aqueducts; they can store it behind dams and release it on demand. But the ground is thirsty. It is thirstier than many people imagine.

Playa lakes are a reminder that all desert water has a lot of dissolved mineral salts in it. Salts in small quantities are nutrients for plants, but in large quantities they are a killer.

The farmer who irrigates his field has to put on enough water to feed his plants and then even more to flush the unwanted salts out of the soil. If he does not, the salts will build up in the soil and it will become saline. Then over the years the yield will get smaller and smaller until no plants can grow.

Farmers are very reluctant to put 'flushing' water on their soils because water is a precious resource. As a result millions of hectares of soil are being ruined from Africa to Australia, from India to Texas.

Huge areas of land have been spoiled
by desertification. Sometimes it is caused by overgrazing, as shown below, on other occasions it has been caused by people cutting the natural vegetation and carrying it away for fuelwood as shown opposite.

Gathering grounds

To poor people living on the edge of the desert, the construction of wells brings the hope that they can survive. It encourages people and their animals to come to the well heads. But this causes disaster because the animals will overgraze lands near a waterhole leaving them at risk of starvation.

The Sahel is the desert edge just south of the Sahara desert. Here people used to be semi-nomadic and had small herds. But their population has risen greatly in the recent past. Each new farmer wants his own herd. To make life easier many more wells were dug to give water for the animals. But this has not helped. It has simply put even more pressure on the sparse vegetation.

Because the plants grow so slowly they cannot cope with the high pressure from grazing. They do not recover, the land cannot support any people and the true desert advances a little more. This is the scourge of the desert margins and it is called desertification.

Killing dunes

People have over-cultivated the poor soils of the desert margins. In doing so they have taken away the protective plants and exposed the already poor soil below. It makes good material for new sand dunes. Today sand dunes are advancing further and further from the true deserts, fed by supplies of soil from fields.

6: A FUTURE FOR DESERTS

The deserts might be daunting places, but they are under a surprising amount of pressure as we have seen. First and foremost, the world's greatest oilfields lie beneath the deserts. The prosperity of the world depends on a continuing supply of this oil. The countries that own it are keen to extract it, and the ruination of the land is seen as a necessary evil. In some of the world's wealthiest countries deserts are ripe for development. The warm winter sun brings people flocking to such areas as soon as they retire. And on the desert margins of the poorest countries hundreds of millions of people are seeking to scratch a living and they have no time to be fussy about how they achieve this.

Everywhere people have always treated the desert as though it was a worthless wasteland, simply fit to dig up and then forget. They have quarried it without worrying about the spoil. They have built nuclear power stations and put hazardous waste dumps all over it. People have even dug up the cacti for their gardens. Only recently have some people begun to care for the land others are spoiling.

Stopping desertification

On the desert margins the population of many developing countries is growing. There are more and more mouths to feed, but no more land to use. The old techniques of land use have caused overgrazing, and some methods of cultivation have led to horrific erosion.

In these places people have to be taught new and simple ways to care for their environment. First and foremost, the people have to find ways of curbing erosion while providing themselves with fuelwood and farmland. To do this effectively they must adopt new techniques, such as building terraces. But they must also learn how to replant dryland trees and shrubs to prevent more erosion. These can be placed where they will not use up valuable farmland. These trees can then eventually be harvested for fuelwood and fodder.

People like this man despair at the sight of desertification. They are anxious to repair the damage if they can be shown how to do it at low cost.

Three pictures on the edge of India's Thar desert *show how to go from disaster to success. In the top picture this tragically eroded land is being lost because the natural plants have been taken away and the ground exposed. But the land can be conserved by using simple techniques. In the second picture Indian farmers are building walls around their fields. When the rains fall the water will not rush over the land and erode the soil but will soak in to the soil and can help make plants grow. The bottom picture shows how the land can be transformed and made green using these simple walls and a small amount of irrigation water applied by hand.*

Homes in the desert

Cities are the largest structures that humans ever create. They are also the biggest consumers of the environment in many ways. This is because we have certain expectations for a comfortable life.

We want power for our homes, water, nearby supplies of groceries and shops to visit. Also we want to be able to drive to visit our friends. In fact the list of needs for a modern family is almost endless. But one thing is certain: in a desert there are none of these things.

Compare the needs of a modern city-dweller with the way that people have lived for centuries in a desert. Their buildings, for example, do not have air conditioning to make them cool: they are built to be airy and light allowing air to circulate freely, or they are built with massive walls to keep the heat of the sun from getting to the rooms. They do not need to use oil, coal or other forms of polluting energy to achieve these things.

Desert mosques owe much of their elegance to the need to design cool spacious interiors for worshippers. By using large windows cool breezes are encouraged without air conditioning.

The traditional way to cope with the desert was to build houses with thick walls and small windows. The building material could be mud because rain falls so infrequently that mud walls will not readily wash away. Settlements like this one were built from the materials in the nearby desert, and they place little demand on the environment.

Dubai is a modern city that has grown up rapidly in the desert. The transformation has been produced by using oil revenues. The intention was to make Dubai look like an important and modern city.

There is no doubt that a modern city has been built. But there have been many environmental penalties from providing modern comforts. The airport, for example, can only be kept free of sand by constant effort and in some cases by pouring tar over the dunes. People live in air conditioned apartments using electricity produced by burning oil.

A modern city demands all modern amenities, such as flush waste disposal. This is Las Vegas in the Nevada desert, USA. The treatment works use huge amounts of water which has to be brought from the River Colorado tens of kilometres away.

Now you start to see the massive task involved in building a modern desert city. Everything has to be brought in and it has to keep on being brought in. It is a mammoth task that takes huge amounts of money and uses enormous amounts of effort and energy.

Living with the desert

Is it possible to live a modern life and not put huge demands on the environment? Certainly better designs of buildings can help. But even air conditioning need not be a drain on energy because desert sunshine is ideal for solar energy conversion.

City environments can be made less demanding by learning to enjoy the natural world. Instead of insisting that open spaces should be green, people can start to appreciate the beauty of desert plants. This is a first step to understanding how they can help care for the desert at quite small cost to themselves and the environment.

Cattle ranching in a desert puts stress on the plant life and costs the country money. One easy way to deal with this abuse of the environment is to remove subsidies paid by the government to the cattle ranchers.

People have always sought to get riches from the rocks. In the desert the climate adds just one more obstacle to the miner's problem: and often the one that kills him. These ghostly remains have stood in this desert for a hundred years, a reminder of when people sweated in the heat to find the mineral borax. The oil fields in Saudi Arabia, shown on the right, are a modern example of mining. In the future people could be made to clear up after they have finished mining rather than leaving the landscape spoiled for centuries to come.

Is there an answer?

People will always want to come to the desert. In the developed world the best way to care for their needs and for the environment is to encourage people to use some areas and not others.

People like desert sun and water, so it is natural to cater for them at lakeside resorts, such as at Lake Mead, USA. If good roads focus on such places then other areas will be less troubled. The desert road shown opposite, bottom left, for example, gets easily flooded. If it is not upgraded then there will be less development in the future.

Desert farming is rarely economical. If the subsidies on farming were removed, many of the worst examples of destruction would disappear. If services were provided less efficiently to outlying settlements, then houses would be less likely to sprawl over desert land, but they would remain in more compact units. And if people visited the desert more often they would begin to appreciate how the desert works and how it should be managed for the future. Caring for the environment is just a matter of understanding.

Cities like Phoenix, Arizona have grown spectacularly. They now demand water which has to be piped from hundreds of kilometres away to supply their thirsty homes. If people had to pay the economic price for such water then the desire to live in the desert would be less.

Desert roads encourage people to use the fragile land more and more. Improving only a few roads will leave other areas less exploited.

Desert sunlight can easily be turned to advantage. This solar-powered street light is just a simple example of how people can become more independent. More solar-powered homes mean fewer utility cables and less disruption to the environment.

A lakeside resort is just the kind of place that could be developed without harming the surrounding environment.

GLOSSARY

aquifer

a rock which has either pores or fissures that allow water to move through it. Most rocks have some water in, but only limestones and sandstones hold enough water to be useful for irrigation

arid zones

those places where the rainfall is very low and unreliable. Arid zones do not have a rainy season and the heat ensures that most of the rain that does fall is quickly evaporated to the air

arroyos

a word for a deep but small gorge

canyon

a deep gorge, often of substantial size and formed in a desert region. There are many regional names for canyons: for example, in North Africa they are called wadis

debris

the broken rock produced as a result of weathering. Debris can be all sizes, but often it accumulates to form a fringe around the base of a cliff

dew

the deposit of water droplets on the surface of vegetation and some other surfaces as a result of overnight cooling of the air

food web

the many animals and plants that live together in a balance, each dependent on the other in some way

high pressure

a region of the Earth's surface where the air sinks. Sinking air stops any cloud forming and prevents rain

oasis

an 'island' of vegetation and human activity in a desert. Oases depend on underground sources of water to provide the springs that sustain them

playa

a salty lake that forms in the centre of a desert basin. It is sometimes filled with rainwater, but for most of the time it is dry with a surface cover of white salt

rainshadow

an area which lies behind a large mountain range which blocks off the flow of moist, rain-bearing winds. As a result rainshadow areas get a reduced rainfall

saline

water which has such a high salt content that it is poisonous to the majority of plants and unfit for people and most animals to drink

saltation

the bouncing and hopping along of sand and small stones as they are caught in a sandstorm

semi-arid

a region near to a desert where the rainfall is enough for significant vegetation to grow and for people to do some farming. Semi-arid regions have a rainy season but the rainfall each season is very unpredictable

siphon

the way in which water can be drawn through a closed tube from one level to another

spate

the state when a river is flowing strongly or is in flood

transpiration

the loss of water from the leaves of plants. This water is drawn out of the soil through the plant roots and this means that transpiration can dry out a soil much more effectively than evaporation

veneer

a thin surface covering of material that masks the rocks of a desert